New Driver's Guide

A Hilarious Handbook for New (and Bad!) Drivers

Wreck-it-Winston

Contents

Introduction

Congratulations! You've studied, passed your written driver's exam, and finally passed the actual driving test *with* an instructor! You are now the proud owner of a driver's license! God help us all. We mean that in the best of ways. But seriously, it's never funny to endanger others with your driving. This book in no way, shape, spirit, or form condones dangerous driving habits.

While there are humorous bits of advice peppered throughout this guide, you should understand that getting behind the wheel of a 2-ton vehicle is serious business. That's about 4,400 pounds of heavy metal in your hands with a driving force capable of hurricane-force-speed over 75 miles per hour (*Estimating wind*, n.d.), and according to the National Weather Service, this type of force can cause "severe and extensive damage. Roofs can be peeled off. Windows broken. Trees uprooted. RVs and small mobile homes overturned. Moving automobiles can be pushed off the roadways." Apply this type of destruction to what you are capable of causing while being behind the wheel of that hurricane. You can imagine the kind of chaos this combination can cause if you are not careful. Do *not* come in like a wrecking ball (McDonald et al., 2013)! Don't be Miley.

An inept driver puts more than their own life at risk with foolish or inattentive driving. Your awesome new car could become a deadly weapon if you steer in the wrong direction for even a fraction of a second. So, while this book is meant to throw light-hearted advice your way, please stay focused when you turn on the ignition of any vehicle.

Take all safety precautions seriously each and every time you get behind the wheel. Hold your friends to this safety code, too. Even if you're not considered the "cool kid" anymore because you follow the rules, at least you won't be the dunderhead driving dangerously. That's not cool!

With nearly 243 million licensed drivers on the road at any given point, according to research done by Hedges & Company, there are bound to be accidents (*How many licensed drivers are there in the US?*, n.d.). Some are fatal. As of 2021, the Centers for Disease Control and Prevention reports that 36,100 people die each year in automotive accidents and that the number one cause of death for individuals ages one year to 54 is being in an accident involving a motor vehicle (*Tips for driving safely during the holiday season*, 2022). Don't become another statistic. You can accomplish the task of safe driving every time by reading and actually *using* the easy-to-follow tips provided here so you don't end up driving like a dumbass or worse.

Chapter 1
What Not to Crash Into

The long and short of this is: everything. You'll want to steer clear of hitting anything you see while on the road and anything you *don't* see. Pedestrians, parked and moving cars, bicyclists, animals, telephone poles, debris like tree limbs, rogue balls rolling out into oncoming traffic, and the children who chase after them. Avoid it all!

Sometimes you cannot see a hazard until it's too late. We get it; you're only human.

Cars and other property are replaceable; humans and pets are not. We could provide a long list of obstacles to avoid while driving on the road, but that would take all day, and we don't have all the space in the world to accommodate such hand-holding. Instead, use common sense—which isn't so common, as it turns out—because you really don't want to hit *anything* while you're driving. It's your most important goal.

The primary objective of driving is to get from Point A to Point B without causing any damage or safety infractions. This isn't *Grand Theft Auto*! There is no point system that rewards your swerving to hit a squirrel or someone crossing the road. Just don't do it!

Swerve away if you need to, or just slow down. Check your mirrors before switching lanes (or swerving) so you don't end up pinballing into the car in your blind spot. Avoiding one accident to cause another is a perfect example of *exactly* how to be a dangerous driver. You're trying to avoid that as much as you're trying to avoid smashing into pieces while driving. As long as you follow these helpful tips, you'll be one step further from being an idiot. Let's get to it!

Keep Your Eyes Moving

Sure, the movies all show whoever is behind the wheel carrying on some serious conversation with their passenger, and they just roll the steering wheel slightly back and forth while keeping their eyes on only one spot in their line of vision. This is totally unrealistic! You'll want to keep your eyes moving from the left of the road to the right, at your speedometer, maybe sneak a glance at your passenger, then to your rearview mirror, side mirrors, and sometimes, you'll need to look over your shoulder when you're changing lanes or reversing.

Don't trust the movies. Everything you see on screen is staged. So, unless you're a multimillionaire celebrity with awesome monologue delivery on some Hollywood set, you'll only have your own set of eyes to rely on when assessing any possible safety hazards, traffic pattern changes, and anything else that could impact your driving as safely as possible (probably) without an audience.

Keep your eyes shifting from one target to the next to avoid any preventable accidents.

But It's Snowing, It's Raining, or Foggy

Get over it, cupcake. Adverse weather happens. Sometimes, you cannot predict when bad weather will happen, even if you're a meteorologist. You know they're usually wrong, anyway. Turn on your windshield wipers and headlights the instant it starts to rain.

You can no more control if you drive on a perfectly sunny spring day while belting out some Britney Spears or if you're down and out miserable, tone deaf, and tearing through "Total Eclipse of the Heart" on a blustery hurricane night with heavy rain. It'll be okay, whatever the weather may be. It can't rain all the time (O'Barr, 1995). But it sure gets foggy sometimes.

Here's a pro tip while driving through fog: Keep your eyes trained on the white shoulder lines (usually) on the right-hand side of the road so that you can approximate where your car is positioned within the lane. This also works when rain makes visibility poor and the lines that separate the lanes of the road impossible to discern. Also, keep your headlights to their normal brightness because using high beams in the fog creates *less* visibility.

Keep your eyes focused on the road and your arms loose, not locked, for the best control of the steering wheel. Wherever your eyes are looking, that is where your hands will subconsciously point the wheel. You guessed it: That's where the tires of the vehicle will point the car, and that will dictate the direction you're heading.

If you begin to skid by hydroplaning through a huge puddle or slip on black ice, turn your wheel *into* the skid. This means you'll need to turn your wheel in the same direction the tail-end of your vehicle is spinning. Slow down when any precipitation begins to fall.

Water and oil don't mix. Until most of the oil that resides on the road has washed away—this can take about 15 minutes—tire traction becomes interrupted by the presence of oil rising to the surface (*First 15 minutes after it rains is most dangerous for drivers*, 2019). So, be especially cautious of taking twisty turns at high speeds when the rain starts. Even a light sprinkle can create hazardous driving conditions.

Give yourself extra travel time. Typically, a good rule of thumb is to keep at least one car length between yourself and the vehicle driving ahead of you. Imagine that there's an invisible car in between you and the other driver ahead of you. It's like when you set your clocks ten minutes ahead of the actual time to trick yourself into arriving at work early. If you can trick yourself into doing this, we've got some lovely real estate in Timbuktu to sell you (wink, wink). Try anyway.

When the rain starts pouring or snow slows your progress, you'll want to keep an additional car's length between you and the probably-a-moron driver in front of you. This extra distance provides additional response time to hit the brakes or steer away from any other possible dangerous moves that could compromise your perfect driving.

So, it's snowing. White death! Oh my, calm down. Breathe. Make sure that you've completely taken all snow and ice off your vehicle before committing to the road. There's no better way to give the driver behind you *Final-Destination* vibes than to keep them guessing if the sheet of solid ice residing on the top of your car will fly off and end them in cinematic gore. You're not transporting lumber, for crying out loud!

You've cleared all the snow from your vehicle, blasted the heat like a furnace, and you're strapped in, toasty, and ready to drive. You've pulled out into traffic, but now you need to stop. Pump your brakes to slow to a gradual stop rather than laying a lead foot on the brake pedal. You'll only cause your car to slip-slide away, or you'll plow into the car ahead of you.

If you must travel when there is a behemoth of snow on the road, use extra caution. Slow down to about 40 miles an hour on the highway and 20 miles an hour elsewhere. Try your best to quell the rabid road rage inside, telling you to pass that slow poke. This will only end with you in a ditch and everyone behind you passing, pointing, and agreeing that you should have known better. At least you'll have given them something to talk about. But you've also created a situation where you're *the* idiot. Don't be an idiot!

Slow Down in Work Sites

The fine for speeding in a work zone, especially for causing bodily injury to roadside workers, increases exponentially. Whenever you see those atrocious orange barrels, cones, and signs while driving, you know it's time to hit the brakes: Softly, of course! There's no need to brake-check the person driving behind you.

Spring and summer months are notorious for construction work on many roadways across the U.S., so be sure you account for this whenever you're driving during these times of the year. Surveyors, utility workers, landscapers, and tree cutters are also busy as bees during the growing seasons when warmer weather invites nature to bloom. Be courteous to everybody working on or near the road. They're risking their lives to provide for their families and to offer necessary public services.

Check Twice for Motorcycles

This should be a given, but as someone who only drives a vehicle with four wheels, you may not think to look out for motorcyclists who share the road with "monster" trucks and semi-trucks that are so much bigger than a tiny two-wheel hog.

With less metal for protection, a motorcycle requires the operator to wear a helmet to keep the cyclist safe (and hopefully bug-free). Who wants to pick bug guts out of your grill? Ew! But seriously, helmets, knee and elbow pads, and even an entire body suit will not be enough to protect the human body from high-velocity impact.

Because you have more protection by being in a larger metal cage on wheels, it will be your responsibility to look out for the little guys. It's your job to check every intersection and lane change *twice* before you move onto the roadways and heinously interrupt what could have been quite an easy ride before you plowed into them. Road rash is painful, but the amount of internal damage a person sustains when they are thrown free from any vehicle at high velocity can be fatal.

Look out for your free-riding road friends by keeping your eyes moving, staying alert, checking twice, and knowing that not everyone shares the road encased in the safety of a four-wheeled cocoon of a car.

Oops!

Now you've done it! We've graciously given you a list of things, people, and objects *not* to hit, but you've gone and hit something anyway. You might be wondering now, *what do I do???* Try very hard to keep calm. Freaking out will only make matters worse.

Admit no fault to anyone. This includes any law enforcement officers, bystanders, or any other parties involved in your big whoopsie. Don't play the blame game. Saying "I'm sorry" or "It's all my fault" only makes you 100% liable for any damages or injuries, even if you aren't completely at fault. Your best bet is to remain calm, ask anyone involved in the accident if they're okay, keep yourself safe, call 911 to get help (and a copy of the police report), and stay beside your vehicle until help arrives.

Never, under any circumstances, flee the scene of an accident. See the section on hit-and-run scenarios for more information.

Exchange insurance information with the other party, personal details like your name and phone number, and make sure you document the location and damage to your car, the other car, or any property by taking pictures! It's always better to be safe than to be sorry. You never know when someone will switch from being a moron to being a jerk, so take as many photos as you can from various angles to protect yourself from future litigation.

Note visually—by taking pictures on your smartphone, drawing a diagram, or writing down—where the vehicle comes to rest. After the incident and cleanup, this step will be important when you review the police report—if there is one. You'll want to check your story against what has been officially recorded, especially for insurance purposes.

Rest assured that your car insurance company will call you. You'll probably end up on a first-name basis with them because they'll be calling you quite a bit as they work with the insurance company of the other party involved in the accident (if there is one).

Expect your insurance premiums to increase. You'll be paying for this slight lapse in judgment for quite some time, even if you weren't the party at fault.

Handy Dandy List If You Have a Whoopsie

You'll want to check each item off this list if you happen to have an accident. This will protect you now and later once the insurance companies start calling you to handle any claims that were filed regarding the accident.

- Have all necessary documents in your car, easily accessible: insurance cards, *valid* (not expired) driver's license, vehicle registration, any inspection info
- Turn off the vehicle, but keep the keys handy.
- Check on your passengers and yourself for any injuries; address these if need be.
- Step out of your vehicle if you are safely able to do so.
- Ask the other driver, or anyone injured, if they are okay.
- Snap some photos of where the car came to a rest after the accident (this includes property, the location of any other vehicles involved, and document any damage to property and vehicles) and where the incident occurred.
- Move your cars out of the road so they aren't obstructing the flow of traffic, if possible.
- Call 911. Cooperate with law enforcement as they note your version of the incident; they will interview anyone else who was involved and witnesses, too.
- Ask the police officer for a copy of the accident report.

- Obtain a copy of the other driver's full name, phone number, home address, car insurance information (company name and policy number), make and model of the vehicles, and license plate numbers.
- Give your information to the other party involved.
- Wait for a tow truck and cleanup crew if your car is totaled or undrivable.
- Call someone to pick you up.
- Once you get home, you'll need to call your insurance company and file a claim to fix any damage to vehicles and property, start a bodily injury claim for any physical injury that occurred, and begin the process of assessing any damages that may mean the car is totaled and you'll need to get a new car.

Hit-and-Run

No one hates an idiot more than a liar. But if you hit someone or something and drive off, leaving the damage behind, you will become a criminal, too. A hit-and-skip, hit-and-run, or dunderhead-and-drive-off is not going to end well for the perpetrator: That's you! With video surveillance becoming the norm in most communities, your chances of having what you didn't want everyone to know you did, going public increases tremendously.

What you should do instead is keep a plastic, resealable baggie with a permanent black marker and a piece of paper in your glove box at all times. This way, if you make a whoopsie and no one is around to see it, you can write a note to the owner of the vehicle or property you damaged using the paper and marker, seal it in the plastic baggie, and secure the package under the windshield wiper of the vehicle or somewhere else the owner will see it.

When you decide to drive away thinking no one saw you, you commit a felony if there were any injuries—because that's the hefty charge likely to be brought against your dumb self when you get caught—you would be wrong. Any safety infraction this severe can carry a one- to seven-year prison sentence, a fine, and loss of driving privileges indefinitely (*New York hit-and-run laws: What to do if a driver leaves the scene*, 2023). This penalty and the charges could vary greatly by state, so be aware of local laws wherever you live and travel. And always do the right thing by calling 911 if someone is hurt or you damage anything that doesn't belong to you.

If you find yourself on the receiving end of a hit-and-run, you'll want to hold the offending party accountable. But never chase them down to do so. It's not the Wild West. There are law enforcement officers assigned to handle these types of cases, so let them do their job. Your job is to document the license plate number (if you can), note the make, model, and color of the vehicle that did the damage, and determine which direction the vehicle was driving before it caused damage and where it went afterward.

Call 911 to report a hit-and-run so that you have a police report to give to your insurance company before you call to make a claim for repairs. You'll need to give all the information you took down when the incident occurred to the police officer who responds and to your insurance company. It's a lot, we know. That's why we already told you not to be an idiot and to be responsible instead if you hit something or someone with your car, even if there were no witnesses. You'd want whoever hit your car to do the same and let you know what moronic thing they did to your vehicle. Do the same for others. As the saying goes: Treat others how you'd like to be treated. Karma can be a...unforgiving force.

Interrupt a Funeral Procession

You might feel encouraged to "speak now or forever hold your peace" at a wedding, but it's incredibly improper to interrupt a funeral. This holds true for the funeral procession, too. When you see a long (or short if the person wasn't liked much) line of cars with their hazard lights blinking and possibly adorned with tiny flags on the driver's side hood, you can bet you're witnessing a person on their way to be laid to rest.

Most states you will drive through in the U.S. have laws that state these types of caravans can drive through red lights as long as they are following the person ahead of them so that the entire group stays together. Out of respect for the person who passed and their mourning friends and family members, don't put the pedal to the metal and cut in at any part of the funeral procession. Respectfully keep your distance.

One of the main points of this long line of cars is to ensure everyone who wishes to say their final farewells can do so. Think of it as a kind of follow-the-leader to get to the final send-off point for their dearly beloved's body.

You certainly don't want to be held responsible for stealing that moment of closure away from anyone, so don't cut in on a funeral procession like an insensitive jerk.

Along the Lines of "Hitting"

Whatever you do, *don't* "hit" that blunt while driving. No drugs or illegal paraphernalia should ever be in your vehicle at any time. Rule number one of safe driving is that you shouldn't drive while under the influence of anything: drugs, alcohol, anger, or stupidity. So, don't be a moron, and don't do drugs (either in or out of the car).

Chapter 2
What Not to Do While Driving

Never take your eyes off the road, even for a moment. Keep your eyes focused on the task at hand. Sure, you might have to sneeze, and you close your eyes for an instant. But anything longer than a sneeze should wait to have your attention until the vehicle comes to a full and complete stop in a safe spot meant for parking. The following list is not exhaustive by any means, so use your best judgment and commit to keeping yourself and others safe by pulling off the road if you need to give anything other than driving your full attention.

Texting

This is a major no-no while you're driving. Even if you're having a huge argument with your partner and you have that one comeback that's going to prove you're right: You're wrong. Pull over out of traffic, park, and then you have all the time in the world to settle the score while texting like your thumbs are on fire. Even glancing at your phone while you're supposed to keep both eyes and hands on their designated targets for optimal road safety can be enough time to miss that the car in front of you has come to a complete halt. Rear-ending someone is not the best way to make new friends.

We highly recommend keeping your phone in your pocket, purse, bag, or otherwise in a hard-to-reach place, out of sight and out of mind. Silence your phone or keep it on vibrate so you aren't also distracted by the notification sounds phone calls, text messages, emails, and apps make. Your life is more important than anything going on online or on your phone. Whatever it is can wait until you are safe and those around you are safe, too.

Road Music

Road music sounds lovely, like you're having your very own music-video-worthy montaging moment. But then a song comes on through the car's stereo system that you wouldn't, in your wildest dreams, have ever chosen yourself, so you just have to change it before your ears bleed. We get it. No one wants to be caught dead listening to Journey with the windows rolled down. Don't let this kind of distraction detract from your attention to your surroundings. Your primary concern while driving is to drive as safely as possible while trying to anticipate if any hazards arise or if other drivers begin making your journey unsafe with their dumbass behaviors. You might be picking a new song by scrolling through Spotify on your phone or hitting the shuffle button like a fiend, but you'll need full focus on the area above your dashboard if you are going to maintain the safety of your driving situation.

It would be best to keep your eyes on the road at all times, with no exceptions. But a safe alternative is to still keep your eyes on the road as you move one hand to change the temperature of your car, the song on the stereo, or adjust your mirrors or seat.

Another, even safer, option is to wait until you are at a full stop at a red light or stop sign to make these adjustments. Pulling over to the side of the road and parking may not always be possible. You could always ignore the discomfort of hearing a bad beat until the next song comes on the radio. Now, that's something that won't kill you even though you might feel like you want to die.

Another strategy might be picking out a playlist to cruise with *before* you pull out of the driveway. Create a playlist or select tracks to go on a queue that will compliment your trek, so you won't be surprised by the bad songs you play. Don't blame us; you picked it!

Feeding Your Face

We get it; you have to eat. Everyday schedules do not always allow adequate time to properly devour a meal at home or even at a table where utensils are needed, and napkins aren't considered a luxury. When you have to eat on the go, skip the condiments. It's impossible to drive and dip safely. But please, do use a napkin because otherwise, your steering wheel will be a disgusting, slippery mess, and you may end up unable to swerve or steer.

Drinking while driving is a HUGE no-no. Of course, this mostly pertains to drinking alcoholic beverages before or during driving. It also means you must use extreme caution when consuming something hot like coffee or tea. If you spill such lava liquids on your lap while driving, not even God Himself can save you from the string of obscenities that will instinctively leave your lips, but there's also the intense burning, too. Avoid scalding yourself by sipping responsibly.

All drinks should have lids to help keep you clean and fire-free and a straw if you're slurping a soft drink or anything cold. Maintain your focus on where you're driving instead of where your drink or food is. You'll need to feel for where you placed these items instead of looking for them. Do this, too, all while keeping one hand firmly on the wheel as you reach.

Any messes you make will require clean-up at your next stop instead of trying to do a sloppy job of sopping up any spills your clumsy self just made. To do this while driving only creates a recipe for disaster. Leave any cleaning up for when you're parked.

Painting Your Face

"You're running late with half your make-up on," or so the song says (Murphy, 2015). You can't go to work looking like a clown, so you start to put on powder, eyeliner, mascara, blush, and lipstick you use to feel more confident about yourself. All of that is okay as long as you aren't driving while doing it. Honestly, applying makeup is an artistic skill that requires your eyes to be trained where the lines are on your face, or you end up coloring outside the lines.

There is no safe way to split your focus between your face and the road while putting on makeup.

Wait until you reach your destination to finish your makeup for everyone's sake. Your beauty regimen can also be completed in the restroom before you reach your desk. And trust us, no one pays *that* close attention to other drivers to notice you aren't wearing either of your fake eyelashes.

Driving While You're Upset

This may seem a bit like overkill, but it's something you may not think about: You should never drive while you're emotionally distressed. The road will be blurry, and your judgment may be cloudy if you drive immediately after receiving bad news. This has been studied extensively: You are 10 times more likely to get into an accident if you are agitated, crying, angry, or sad (Dockrill, 2016). Your reaction time may be negatively impacted or delayed by the same emotional distractions that may make you feel more willing to engage in risk-taking behaviors like running red lights or speeding.

The best thing you can do if you need to go somewhere when you're incredibly upset is to sit behind the wheel with the car off until you feel calmer. Collecting your emotions, regaining control, and wiping your eyes clear of tears will help you drive more cautiously than if you begin driving without dealing with your emotions first. You can calmly select any mood music that will help you "de-Hulk" on the way to your destination. Turn off your phone until you're parked again, Bruce.

Speeding through your heartache and rage won't do anything other than end in disaster. So, don't pass this pain on to your family and friends because you chose to drive under the influence of an agitated state.

Don't Make Us Turn This Car Around!

We're guessing since you're a new driver that you probably aren't a new parent, too. But hey, maybe you're babysitting. Maybe you just needed a refresher course on safe driving. Either way, you should know kids can be incredibly distracting while you're driving.

They throw things, including tantrums, and you may feel the need to reach back and teach them to quiet down the old-fashioned way. But don't do this. Your hands, attention, and eyes are likely to leave the field of vision that requires frequent scanning, and you may end up in a car accident.

If you find your tiny wards misbehaving or there is a spill to clean up, just take a very deep breath. Remember the eating while driving rule? That applies to feeding kids in the car, too, but for whatever reason, you broke this rule, so here you are... just breathe. You can clean up whatever mess there is when you reach your destination.

If the kids are crying, fighting, or getting out of their car seats or seat belts, you may need to pull off the road to have a calm discussion with little Timmy while you strap him back into the car. It's never okay to distract the driver, and throwing objects does just that. Teach them while they're young, too, that each car ride, no matter how short in duration or distance, requires the same level of utmost safety. This means wearing a seatbelt for every ride, with no exceptions. You should set the perfect example by donning your safety belt for every car ride, as well, whether you are the driver or not.

Unfortunately, you may have to pull over several times on multiple occasions for these lessons to stick. But it is imperative to keep to your principles each and every time.

Don't Play Behind the Wheel

It might be tempting to pretend to swerve or jerk the wheel while your friends are in the car. *Don't do this!* Ever! While it may end in a bout of hilarious laughter, it could also end in someone getting extremely hurt or dead. You could even end up being responsible for damaged property. So, the best thing to do when you're being dared to do something stupid is: Don't do it. Dare them to be a good friend, and you do what you know is the right thing to do. Protect the people in and out of your vehicle by making the smart choice to conscientiously drive cautiously so that you don't become a liability.

Obstruction of Your Line of View

Bumper stickers are cool and all: You let the entire world know exactly how you feel about any kind of issue facing humanity today. Driving is about individuality and independence, after all. Bumper stickers are meant to go on the bumper, where you aren't required to maintain an optimal visual field of your surroundings because bumpers aren't see-through. The one thing you *do not* want to do is plaster so many stickers across your vehicle's rear, front, and side windows that you cannot see out of them.

This is pure moron behavior and can lead to unnecessary blind spots. Do not limit your field of vision in the name of activism. You can love veganism until the cows come home, but you never want to turn your car into a moving billboard just to plow into someone or something because you got a bit overzealous with the decorations. There are better ways to help your cause than to deface and make a dangerous situation out of your car.

Keep rear-view mirror decorations to a minimum, too. We're looking at you who accessorize and smell-ify everything with Yankee Candle air fresheners and dazzling, dangling crystals. It's cool to celebrate your individuality, too, but let's not go overboard to the point that it interferes with your ability to see out of every window at every inch of your surroundings.

Keep your field of vision in peak performance by limiting any accessories inside and out of your vehicle.

Don't Drive Without Medical Clearance

This can seem like a no-brainer, but if you've had recent surgery or are in so much pain that you require the use of narcotic or sedating pain medication to function, you should not be operating heavy machinery. Cars are heavy machinery. When your body is focused on healing, your mind is not going to be fully operational enough to maintain physical flexibility or mental sharpness. Your reflexes may be negatively impacted, so your response time to road hazards will diminish. This can put you, your passengers, and others in danger.

Make sure you're also reading about any adverse effects of other medications because these can also affect your motor functions. Allergy medicines are notorious for causing drowsiness and clouded thinking. If you're starting a new medication and the label states that it may cause drowsiness or impaired motor function, you should take the medicine when you know you won't be driving anywhere any time soon. This way, you are able to discern any side effects that might make it difficult or dangerous for you to drive *before* you even try it.

You may need that gallon of milk from the store, but you should have someone else take to the road and bring it to you instead. Never defy doctor's orders, especially when it comes to being physically able to operate a moving vehicle. Even the shortest trips can cause catastrophic consequences. And that's not funny at all.

Futz With the GPS

Sometimes, you'll find yourself arguing with an electronic... No, you're not crazy. You're just like the millions of other Americans—more accurately, that's 60% of U.S. users—who rely on a global positioning system (GPS) electronic device to help navigate where the hell you're going so that you get there on time (*Study reveals where drivers are most reliant on their GPS*, n.d.).

Gone are the days of printing out MapQuest directions as you bounce between reading the directions in hand and driving your dinosaur downtown. Don't let this technological advantage take you down a golf course, rolling over golf balls and sending them flying like tiny cannon balls across the green. Just because an electronic know-it-all told you to take that left turn in Albuquerque, that doesn't mean the AI machine has accurately accounted for the contingencies of road closures, traffic accidents, road hazards, new construction, or re-routed traffic. Humans are fallible; technology is worse!

Waze and Siri might have you pulling a U-turn into some high security top secret government roadway because the satellite your navigation app is pinging from operates under the assumption that you're on the correct road when, no sir, you most definitely are not!

Use your common sense, gut instinct, intuition, best judgment, and eyes to tell you your GPS AI is wrong.

There is no use arguing with it. It's imperfect and will offer the wrong information from time to time. You can yell back all you want, but that sucker is programmed (by you) before you begin to put your vehicle in motion so that it keeps rerouting no matter how many times you pass up the opportunity to take the first right at the next stoplight.

If you find the jibber-jabber distracting, then, by all means, mute it! Change the lighting effects, color scheme, and font size to suit your best visibility at a glance because that's all you should be doing: glancing from time to time to calculate your next move. Never futz with the GPS or fiddle with the positioning of the device while you're actively driving. Wait until you've parked away from obstructing moving traffic so that you can give your full attention to the road while driving and to your GPS when you need to manually reroute the little bugger because it's irritated you off one too many times.

Have everything you need, all your electronics and music, situated before you put your car into gear. It should be one less thing to distract you from safe driving. Keep it that way by following these tips to ensure the safest, shortest, easiest route to wherever you're going. And always avoid driving on the green.

Chapter 3
How Not to Deal With Other Drivers

Racing and road rage: Ah, the great American pastimes of our ailing grandparents. It's a good thing everyone grows up, even as a society, and these are no longer socially acceptable ways to prove someone is a "man" or winner. Playing chicken by aiming your vehicle at your opponent's vehicle and swerving at the last second to prove you're not a "chicken" is also a big no-no. These could put you, your friends, any bystanders, and tons of peripheral property in harm's way.

Please operate any vehicle responsibly by keeping your eyes on the road, limiting the road rage to a fabulous string of obscenities that never leave the inside of your car, and keeping both hands on the steering wheel. No matter how tempting it is to ram the car that just cut you off, the insurance premiums alone should be enough to talk you out of it. Do you really want to hurt yourself? We're not even going to ask about the other guy.

Streets of Rage

More than just an awesome 90s video game, the concept of keeping your rage off the road has become quite the issue for most drivers who have spent any amount of time driving lately. You might be surprised to learn that Utah has some of the most confrontational drivers on the road. If you're from Utah, you probably already know this. You may be further surprised to learn that New York state (coming in towards the bottom of the list at 46th) doesn't have as many aggressive drivers as the supposedly-chill Colorado residents (who rank third), midwestern Missouri (which ranks second), and—you guessed it—Utah ranks first on the list of states when it comes to the number of drivers who let their emotions get the best of them while driving (Lobb, 2022).

Whatever the circumstances may be when you find yourself with steam coming out of your ears and your temper flares while you're driving, the very best thing you can do is CHILL. Take as many deep breaths as you need until your blood pressure and intense feelings of sabotage, decrease. It doesn't matter *why* you caused the accident; if you're angry at another driver and cause an accident, especially on purpose because you're angry, you will still be liable for damages.

So, keep the road rage to those simulated video games where there are do-overs. Life has no reset buttons, and you're going to regret any life choices made while enraged.

Speed It Up

When you're driving in residential areas, it's probably a good idea to keep your eyes searching for a speed limit sign. These parts of each neighborhood (where people live) tend to have signs posting safe speeds of 20 to 35 miles per hour. Never go above these limits, or you risk harming children who might be playing outside.

You'll notice that this section is named "Speed It Up," that's a very astute observation. You're learning already. This is because there are a few scenarios where speed is your friend. For instance, on the highway, interstate, or other fast-moving thruways, you need to keep the speed of the vehicle you're driving above 45 miles per hour.

So, speed up, slowpoke! And stay in the furthest right-hand lane except to pass vehicles driving more slowly than you are or to make room for stalled vehicles on the shoulder.

Slow Down!

You'll need to speed up on the highway, but driving over the speed limit anywhere is for dummies. You are 13 times more likely to cause an accident if you are speeding (Dockrill, 2016). Any amount over the posted speed limit carries this risk. However, we'll state the obvious by telling you that the faster you drive above the speed limit, the likelihood of you causing an accident also increases in tandem. This is why you may find yourself being pulled over by a police officer if you are caught speeding.

Of course, you don't want to risk getting your first speeding ticket. The entire experience of getting pulled over by law enforcement officers can be nerve-wracking and expensive! We'll cover this topic more in-depth in the next chapter, but here is a word of caution about being a speed demon: Don't. Don't go more than five miles over the posted speed limit. It's never worth it.

Going faster doesn't always get you to your destination any faster, but it sure can wrack up points against your license, hundreds of dollars in fines, and an increased car insurance premium. Skidding to a stop at traffic lights that have turned red will damage the treads on your tires, brakes, brake pads, rotors, engine, and transmission. Not to mention that your gas mileage will deplete faster than the ozone layer.

Make Up Your Mind

Speed up, slow down...Which should you do? As the captain of your vehicle navigating concrete streets like they were majestic seas, the speed at which you travel is your decision. But you alone must live with the consequences. Like a bad haircut with bangs, the way you drive your car could end up defining you. Maybe your mom won't set foot in the car if you're driving because you curse like a sailor whenever the lights are too long. Maybe your spouse rolls their eyes so loud you can hear them rattling in their head above the slow hum of the painfully slow car you're driving.

Use common sense discretion to determine the speed you should maintain. Switch it up as you pass through different zoning areas (residential, city, country, highway, etc.) so you don't get pulled over or your ship goes out of control. You can't control what others will think about your driving ability, but you *can* control your temper (a la sans the road rage), and you *can* leave the reckless driving and evasive maneuvers to your video games.

It's Called a "Turn Signal" for a Reason

Dispelling the mystery here: it's called a "turn signal" because you're supposed to *signal* your turn *before* you turn! It's a magical, mystical concept that escapes many drivers, and it can be infuriating when you have to slam on your brakes to avoid a fender-bender. Even in this scenario (as with any other scenario that ends with your bumper in the car-ahead-of-you's business), you will be cited for causing the accident: just because you were the car behind the damaged vehicle!

This is also why leaving enough space between you and the driver ahead of you is well-advised. So, always use your turn signal (also known as an indicator) for every turn, and don't rely too heavily on the driver ahead of you always using theirs. It's up to you to stop in enough time to avoid smacking into their rear end.

Arriving at a Four-Way Stop

So, you're at a four-way stop where each of the four drivers has a stop sign, and you don't know what to do. You're in luck because you're about to learn!

First, you should never assume that another driver is going to give you the right of way. Most people out there on the roads are a bunch of jerks (not you, of course), but the safest bet is to give other drivers the right of way first. Then, look for your opportunity to make a safe move into traffic. This means you'll need to anticipate what directions the other drivers present are going to go, and you will fit yourself in accordingly. This is also known as defensive driving, the opposite of offensive driving. Not "offensive" like you're cruising around cursing at people, but "defensive" like you're defending your right to drive safely against other drivers who choose to drive aggressively. You're protecting yourself and your passengers.

If the power is out at an intersection, and the stop lights don't work, never fear! Use the four-way stop rules you just learned to navigate this roadblock. The official rule is that the drivers turning right without crossing the center of the intersection have the right of way. So, turning right from the right lane gives these drivers the right of way. Anyone trying to turn left needs to yield to other drivers who are driving straight or making a right-hand turn, and then you'll each take turns in a counter-clockwise circle. Continually keep your eyes moving for any potential collisions that could occur as you travel through the interaction during your turn. You can never be *too* cautious. Other drivers are too unpredictable.

It's better to drive defensively; think of a linebacker looking for the tiniest tell about what their opponent is about to do, then making their move to avoid it. Even if the oncoming car has its turn signal on, there is no guarantee that they didn't just forget it was ticking away and left it blinking like an oblivious idiot. Wait until they begin to make their move before you make yours. You'll prevent so many unnecessary collisions this way.

Times When You're *Not* the Idiot Driver

Believe it or not, there will be times when you won't be the idiot driver slowing everyone down or speeding around garbage trucks. So, how do you deal with someone that is infuriating you without putting the pedal to the metal and ramming their rear end?

The first thing you're going to want to do is to imagine yourself sitting next to them in their car, your hands around their neck. Nope. Don't do this. Focus on the road. Internally, focus on your breathing. Try to breathe deeply and evenly. Count your breaths if you must, but the end goal is to get your heart rate back under manageable parameters and not at the height of fight or flight.

This stress reaction, where your nervous system perceives a threat and reacts by releasing adrenaline through your bloodstream, is responsible for keeping your instincts sharp in preparation for saving your life in dangerous situations. Don't create a situation that requires your body to defend itself, however. Avoid bodily harm by keeping your body in your own car.

You may have heard that individuals under such duress are able to lift a car with their bare hands! Don't bet on it, but you will get a rush of superhuman abilities like greater observation as you scan your environment for clear paths to escape, and your grip might tighten on the wheel in preparation for evasive maneuvering in case the idiot in front of you slams on their breaks or spins wildly out of control.

If the situation progresses and the other driver gets out of their car to address you personally, de-escalate any confrontational situation by keeping your emotions in check. If at any point the driver of the other vehicle exits their car, roll up all the windows and carefully drive yourself away from the moron in question.

You don't need to engage in any macho-man, she-woman backroad brawls to prove whose carburetor is bigger. It's not worth it. You've got somewhere more important to be. You'll get there much faster if you keep your eyes on the prize or better yet: the road.

The absolute best way to diffuse an already heated situation is to match the other party's crazy with your own personal calm. This mostly pertains to situations where you cannot drive away (like if you're stuck in some less-than-epic traffic jam). Make it a point to whisper or lower your voice, especially if they're yelling. Bringing your voice down to a lower volume ensures they have to be quieter to hear what you're saying.

Also, keep a safe distance away from anyone who seems out of control. The closer your face is to them, the more likely they are to start swinging. Maintain enough space to convey respect. Maybe you should just stay in your car unless it's absolutely imperative that you exit your vehicle. You have to go to work or school, but you want to get there in one unpulverized piece.

Be like your parents when you ask for an allowance: ignore to the best of your ability when someone is being exceptionally annoying. Not that you are, that is. No, you're exceptional.

Chapter 4
Avoiding Tickets and Accidents

Keep your eyes on the road, your surroundings, and your speedometer: in that order. Both of your hands should be on the steering wheel at all times. Whether it's the classic ten-and-two hand position on the wheel or some variation, it's best to hold the steering wheel with both hands. That's 100% control versus the reduced 50% you might get by using only one hand. It's not rocket science or even algebra; it's just common sense.

One hand on the steering wheel is better than using your knee and the grace of God to steer, but you already know that when you use two hands, you have greater control over your 2-ton death metal on wheels. It just makes sense: More hands equal more control. But you only need two! Your passengers should keep their hands to themselves while you're in the driver's seat. Don't be the jerk who jerks the wheel!

Wear your seatbelt, and you should enjoy a safe journey. Right? You're going along smoothly, enjoying your Saturday luxury ride, until a rogue deer runs out in front of your unsuspecting headlights in the dead of night. These things cross the road like they've got some personal vendetta, and your car in particular is standing in the way.

It's never fun to hit an animal. Bambi and Thumper never did anything to hurt anyone, but nature is cruel. Animals and children don't have the wherewithal to understand the dangers involved in crossing any roads. Night driving makes visibility low; if any kind of precipitation is falling, it makes seeing certain dangers that much trickier.

So how do you avoid being the bad guy in such a lovely Disney-woodland-creature story or being pulled over by Officer Friendly? We're so glad you asked; here's how.

Skip to the Good Part

Okay, the title of this section is a lie. Being pulled over by any authority figure is never a good or fun scenario. But you can bet that it will happen at some point to you during your lifetime as a driver. Probability is not in your favor here. It's just something that you need to plan for *when* it happens. So, what should you do when you see those red and blue flashing lights tailing you?

First, you'll want to slow your vehicle and check your rearview mirror a couple of times, in between keeping your eyes on the road, to make sure you're the driver being pulled over. Turn on your right blinker to indicate to the officer that you are aware you need to pull to the shoulder of the road. Gradually bring your vehicle to a slow stop.

Remain calm. We cannot emphasize this enough. Now is not the time to prove to your fellow passengers how much of a moron you are. Trust us, they already know.

Cooperate with everything the officer tells you to do *exactly* as they tell you to do it. Keep your hands visible. Make no sudden movements. And refrain from using any obscenities. Maintain a respectful manner of speaking and be polite.

In the amount of time it takes for the officer to run your plates and determine if your tags are up-to-date, you'll need to begin gathering all the documentation the officer will likely ask you to provide *before* they approach your vehicle (probably from the driver's side). You should also turn off your car, turn off any music being played, and collect all your documents to give to the officer. This will be your license, driver's license, proof of car insurance (if your state requires it), vehicle registration, and possibly proof of current state inspection for your vehicle, depending on the registration requirements by the Department of Motor Vehicles where you live. If you're driving a rental car, you'll need to provide the receipt and any temporary insurance you purchased when you took out the rental.

Next, you will turn off your vehicle engine. Roll your window down to have a calm discussion with the officer who stopped you. Greet them politely. Be aware of your hands; keep them visible on the steering wheel except to slowly offer them the documents you've gathered. Once you have given the officer everything they asked for, they will probably return to their vehicle to check your license for points against your driving record and run a search for any outstanding warrants. Being ready to greet the officer with all pertinent documents they will *definitely* ask you to produce goes a long way in keeping you protected from an unnecessary escalation of force and being asked to step out of the vehicle for a possible search.

If you are stopped by a police officer at night, you will want to turn on any interior lights to avoid having a flashlight shined in your eyes. Even cops can't see at night.

This is also why you'll want to have both of your hands resting on the steering wheel, where the police officer can see them at all times. If you are instructed to reach for additional documents, do so with the utmost care as if you are moving in slow motion. This will help the officer track your movements as non-threatening.

Here's the most important part: If you do have some sort of weapon in the car (like a gun or a knife), you will need to let the officer know ahead of time. You'll probably be asked, "Do you know why I pulled you over today?" And you can respond with "yes," "no," or "I'm not sure," but the next pause in the conversation needs to be when you address the elephant in the room by saying, "Just so you are aware, officer, I do have a firearm in my trunk. It's not loaded." Be honest about any drugs or open canisters of alcohol you may have in your possession, as well. Any dishonesty will go against you in the worst way. Be proactive when addressing anything that the officer could perceive as threatening or illegal so that you are able to keep yourself and your passengers safe.

Protect yourself. It is deeply regrettable that the risk of being a victim of police violence has increased to affect every 1 in 1,000 Black men, and most individuals, regardless of race, gender, or ethnicity, between the ages of 20 and 35 (Edwards, Lee, & Esposito, 2019). With that being said, you'll be scared. You may have shaky hands, a shaky voice, and be sweating profusely. Take some deep breaths. Try to explain your actions to the best of your ability, even when you're nervous. But never run from the police. This puts a target on your back, unfortunately, sometimes literally.

Please inform the officer of any move you are about to make before you make it and even while you make your move. You can never be too cautious. While the officer has your documents, look for a badge number or the officer's last name in case you may need this information later. Make a mental note. You can write it down or text it to yourself once the incident is over and the officer is on their way.

You may have heard that you can refuse a voluntary search of your vehicle. While there are a few people who might be able to argue their way out of this scenario, it would be worth it to keep your safety a priority and comply with what the officer is asking. Maybe you have something questionable in your vehicle—while it would be prudent to keep such items out of your car whenever you're on the go, it's not always the way things work out—but don't let the presence of such items be what escalates the situation.

Whether you're in or out of your vehicle, keep your hands visible at *all* times. This means you'll freeze your fingers off in frigid weather, but you'll be able to walk away from the interaction (hopefully) unharmed. No hands in your pockets, no searching through your purse, and no sudden turns to grab anything out of your car!

Remember: Most officers (at least enough of them) operate under the assumption that you are a threat. This does not make them the enemy. Their primary job is to enforce the laws passed by people in legislation, to keep civilians safe, and maintain peace. Anything they deem out-of-the-ordinary or too quick will trigger their fight or flight response, and generally speaking, police officers aren't trained to flee from a fight. You may startle them into pulling their gun.

Explain what you are retrieving *before* you begin to reach. And reach slowly when you do.

Never argue with an officer, but you should instead take up any complaints about the encounter with a judge when the court date arrives. This date should be printed on any tickets the officer writes (they will definitely hand you a copy), and there should be a phone number to call where you can seek help in answering any questions you might have about the ticket, fine, charges, or anything else you might need.

Your goal is to have the shortest, safest interaction possible with any law enforcement officer you encounter and be able to drive away to live another day afterward.

High Beams and Headaches

Now that the unpleasantness is out of the way, we'll discuss ways to avoid accidents. There are some states that you may drive through that require you to have your headlights on during precipitation events and at dusk, dawn, and during the night. Failing to flip on these lights is a dead giveaway for local law enforcement to pull you over. Instead of a deer in headlights, you're an idiot without headlights on!

If the sun is too bright, you can opt to wear sunglasses during the day. But never be so cool, like the song implies, and wear your sunglasses at night. Even if you find that all the lights look like splayed stars, or you have a massive headache, you should never drive at night while wearing shades. This makes visibility poor, so you may not spot pedestrians, parked cars, wild animals, or mailboxes very well in the added dimness.

With 75% of accidents taking place at intersections, you'll want to keep especially vigilant wherever roads meet (*Motorists & parking: Street safety tips*, 2023). Check, then double-check for pedestrians crossing the road and walking in the crosswalk. Give the right of way to pedestrians, bicyclists, and motorcycle riders. Pro tip: Look left, then right, and then look left once more before lifting your foot off the brake pedal. Search areas you would expect to find anyone walking, running, or biking so that you can avoid them like an expert introvert.

Under no circumstances should you ever veer left of center. This means never crossing the double yellow lines that separate your lane from that of oncoming traffic. This is a very fast way to end up dead, especially at high speeds.

If you're too sick to drive, please call an Uber or let someone else drive you.

Speeding Straight to Jail

Not instantly, of course, but if you're driving more than 10 miles per hour over the posted speed limit, or you're driving recklessly (sure, it sounds like wreck-less is a good thing, but we promise you it won't end well), you're going to trigger a chance encounter with a police officer and accrue some fines in the meantime. You may end up hearing sirens wailing, seeing lights revolving red and blue, and being pulled over by a law enforcement officer who's incredibly eager to hand you your very first speeding ticket.

These come with hefty fines and possible points added to your license that go on your permanent driving record. Accumulate enough of these points, and you'll find yourself with a suspended license. Try to learn from the first infraction. Slow down, take your time, and try not to panic. This isn't *Star Trek*; there is no warp speed. No one will applaud your panic at the disco or on the road. The only "trophy" you may end up "winning" is a paper copy of a summons to appear in court so that you can be assigned and fined the corresponding amount for however many road safety no-nos you violated. The faster you go over the legal speed limit, the higher the fine will be.

Rolling, Rolling, Rolling Stops

When you come to a stop sign, you might be tempted to "play the game in pause mode," where you pause at the intersection, but you don't actually stop. The po-po is watching your every move. This kind of rolling stop, where your vehicle remained in motion when it was supposed to suspend motion, will get you a ticket for sure! Take it from a pro-roller.

Just because you don't get fined every time you roll through a stop sign doesn't mean that karma won't catch up to you. The next time could be when Officer Karma rips you a ticket and a hole in your wallet.

The best thing you can do to ensure this does not happen to you is to come to a complete stop at each and every stop sign along your route. Look left, right, and look left again before pulling out into traffic once more. You should use this three-second stop to look out for other moving vehicles, pedestrians, bicyclists, motorcyclists, and other possible hazards you might hit if you hadn't fully paused at this juncture.

Avoid Getting Pulled Over

There's no foolproof formula to avoid ever being pulled over by an officer of the law, but your best bet is to obey all traffic rules. This means drive the speed limit or a bit under, come to a complete stop at all stop signs and wait three seconds before pulling out into traffic, wear your seat belt for every ride, keep your hands off your electronics, never drive inebriated or while sleepy, and avoid hitting all obstacles. Easy peasy.

You may be tempted to drive at a higher speed if you are late for work. This will likely end in you being pulled over, running even later than you were if you have only driven at or slightly below the speed limit.

When Your Car is the Problem

There's no failsafe way to *not* be an idiot while driving other than to do your best. Sometimes, you end up the villain in other people's stories, no matter how much good you put out into the world. Remember karma? Karma doesn't always play fair. You can't control what others think about you, but you can control how safely you drive your vehicle. "Only *you* can prevent forest fires!" (*The story of Smokey the Bear*, 2014). Be honest; you read that with your chest puffed, hands on your hips, and in your best, deep Smokey the Bear voice, didn't you? The sentiment is the same: Only *you* can prevent your driving like a moron!

So, keep gas in your tank, oil in your engine, tread on your tires, stay up-to-date on all state inspections for your vehicle, and maintain an overall healthy transportation machine to avoid inadvertently being the idiot and causing a wreck with your less-than-stellar clunker. When your tire tears away from the rim it's been sitting on since it was built, and you lose control, or your brake light stays silent when it should be on alert, that's all your fault (not amoré).

Any maintenance issues with your car that cause an accident to occur point the finger at you, and now you're liable for any damage this inattentiveness has caused. The technical term is being negligent. And you do not want to be it! Prevent any liability in these instances by conducting monthly mainte-nance checks and ensuring any repairs are made before you drive again.

You Brake for Animals

Go, you! You're a steward to the entire planet, but there's a bit of a catch. Before you go playing Robin Hood in the merry forest or Snow White talking to tiny woodland creatures, you'll want to make sure there is no one behind you who will have no idea what you're up to and, therefore won't be able to stop in enough time to keep from pushing you into the very animals you're trying to save in the first place. This is also why you don't want to tailgate the vehicle ahead of you. They could also be a tree-hugging hippy, like you, and stomp the brake in hopes that every chicken crossing the busy highway in front of them makes the safe journey to the other side. So, there you have it: The real reason the chicken crossed the road is because some altruistic superhero stopped two lanes of traffic so that it could. Mystery solved!

If you see movement at the side of the road, a reflection of eyes in the woods, or a single whitetail deer, you can safely assume that you need to slow down. Where you see one deer, often-times, there will be more that follow. You can try to flash your high beams at oncoming drivers to alert them of the situation, but this isn't always a foolproof warning system. Turn on your hazard lights until the path is clear to begin driving again to help drivers who approach you see that you are stopped in the roadway. Otherwise, you will have done all you can to help the animal cross as safely as possible.

But nature is cruel, as we've explained earlier. Not every animal is fortunate enough to cross the path of someone so selfless every time it needs a drink of water or returns to its den for the night. Then, there are other times when you are unable to stop, regardless of how much you want to, because the laws of physics are not on your side. Science works the way it works regardless of your feelings, and momentum is hard to correct when you're going at increased speeds.

This may counter what you might have heard from your high school gym class teacher/driving instructor on nights and weekends, but you are never supposed to plow into any animals that cross your path. Doing so does *not* create a safer or more controlled crash; it just makes the entire situation worse...and messier. But if you are unable to stop and you collide with Bambi, your first concern is to move your vehicle off the road where other drivers won't hit you. You don't want to add to the mayhem.

You also don't want to slam on your brakes. This will make you lose control of the vehicle and cause any drivers behind you to slam into you. It will be much worse than a simple fender bender!

Call 911 and take care of any injuries you or your passengers may have sustained. This is a good time to mention how having a first aid kit in your vehicle can be a lifesaver. Keep it stocked with medical supplies and road flares. And check if you need to restock whenever you do your monthly vehicle inspection.

Look for the animal with your eyes, but never chase or try to approach it. It's not called "wildlife" because it's tame. There's probably nothing you can do to save the animal. When you call for emergency assistance, you should also mention that you struck an animal so that they can provide help for them, too. Don't expect life-saving measures for the creature, but they will do what is right for the animal, so it doesn't have to suffer.

When the unthinkable happens, and you've done all you can do but accidentally hit someone's pet, you'll probably want to help in any way you can. But do this safely if you must. Animals who are in pain are more likely to lash out by clawing and biting. If you can see a name or number on the collar without touching the injured pet, that's fantastic. Otherwise, you should call a local animal control agency for assistance from someone who is trained in how to handle animals safely, and they can notify the owner for you.

If there is damage to your vehicle or someone else's property, you will also need to call your insurance company to file a claim. Brace yourself because the hike in premiums could also throw you into a tailspin.

School Is in Session

Warm summer days give way to crisp autumn mornings, and then suddenly, you see a slew of vibrant yellow school buses causing congestion on your morning commute and your nightly drive home. So, what gives? Everyone has to share the road, right? So why, you may be wondering, do all these annoying school buses get the right of way and take up so much road space, including making *huge* wide turns?

The answer is simple, moron: because they cart dozens of delicate children to and from school each and every day of the week (except holidays and weekends, God bless them). School bus drivers are underrated saints. If you've spent any amount of time driving near a school bus with your windows rolled down, you know firsthand how rowdy a group of middle schoolers can be.

They're throwing paper airplanes and shoes out the window, thinking it's hilarious. But this causes unsafe driving conditions for any drivers nearby and for the bus driver, too. Their main concern is ensuring the safety of the children in their car while simultaneously keeping their calm under intense pressure. Parents and school boards can be a real drag!

The best way to approach a school bus is to maintain a safe distance from them at all times. The standard length is about 500 feet of distance between you and the school bus ahead of you. Search for any signs of flashing lights or the extension of a stop sign attached to the driver's side of the bus to signal that the bus is about to stop, and children will depart.

Here is the tricky part: When do you stop for school buses as children exit? The ultimate answer is each and every time you see those lights flashing and children crossing: You stop. Oncoming traffic: Stop. You're behind the bus: You stop. You're stopped at a side street, but you want to pull out into traffic ahead of the bus: *You stop*! If you think hitting a deer is devastating, you can only imagine how horrible it's going to feel if you fail to stop when a child is crossing the road.

That's not funny at all. So, don't be a jerk or idiot, and slow down whenever you see children playing. Stop completely whenever a school bus is loading or unloading students. You'll save the future this way, and you'll save yourself a lot of heartache, too.

Conclusion: No Excuse to Drive Like an Idiot

By this point, you have absolutely no excuse if you're found driving like an ignoramus. This book has covered all the major mistakes first-time drivers could possibly make. You should have committed this comprehensive, so-easy-even-a-child-could-do-it (if it wasn't illegal for children to drive) guide to road safety to memory.

Keep your eyes open and focused on the road. Try to avoid causing an accident or driving like an aggressive great white shark in a demolition derby full of guppies. Never drink and drive or be in a vehicle where the driver (including you) is under the influence of any mind-altering substance. If you're too tired to drive home, pull over or ask someone to pick you up. Don't drive if you're tired or agitated.

Wear your seat belt for every trip, no matter how short the distance or duration.

Take your vehicle into a trusted auto body shop for a safety inspection once every year, but conduct an informal safety check yourself every month. Have the oil changed in your vehicle, and check your brake lights, headlights, windshield wipers, and other functions to maintain the safety and longevity of your vehicle.

You now know all the ways to keep yourself and others safe as you enjoy your newfound freedom through driving. Be the considerate, defensive driver that lets other drivers merge in front. And whatever you do, don't drive like an idiot.

Bibliography

Animals on the road: 10 expert tips to reduce your chances of a serious accident. (2023). Driving Tests. https://driving-tests.org/beginner-drivers/how-to-avoid-animals-on-the-road/

Dockrill, P. (2016, February 26). *Driving while angry or sad increases your risk of crashing by nearly 10 times.* Science Alert. https://www.scienceal ert.com/driving-while-angry-or-sad-increases-your-risk-of-crashing-by-nearly-10-times

Driver safety. (2004). New York State DOT. https://www.dot.ny.gov/programs/driver-safety

Driving tips. (n.d.). New York State DOT. https://dmv.ny.gov/older-driver/driving-tips

Education & safety. (2023). Wildlife NYC. https://www.nyc.gov/site/wildlifenyc/animals/education-safety.page

Edwards, F., Lee, H., and Esposito, M. (2019, August 5). *Risk of being killed by police use of force in the United States by age, race-ethnicity, and sex.* PNAS. https://www.pnas.org/doi/10.1073/pnas.1821204116

Estimating Wind. (n.d.). National Weather Service. https://www.weather.gov/pqr/wind

First 15 minutes after it rains is most dangerous for drivers. (2019, July 11). WWSB Channel 7 News. https://www.mysuncoast.com/2019/07/11/tips-driving-safely-inclement-weather/

How many licensed drivers are there in the US?. (n.d.). Hedges & Company. https://hedgescompany.com/blog/2018/10/number-of-licensed-drivers-usa/

Lightner, C. (2017). *The top ten best driving practices.* We Save Lives. https://wesavelives.org/the-top-ten-best-driving-practices/

Lobb, J. (2022, September 12). *States with the most confrontational drivers, ranked.* Forbes Advisor. https://www.forbes.com/advisor/car-insurance/state-rankings-confrontational-drivers/

McDonald, M., Moccio, S., Skarbek, S., Kim, D., Gottwald, L., and Cirkut. (2013). Wrecking Ball [Recorded by Miley Cyrus]. On *Bangerz* [Album]. RCA.

Motorists & parking: Street safety tips. (2023). New York City DOT. https://www.nyc.gov/html/dot/html/about/street-safety.shtml

Bibliography

Murphy, M. (2015). Greek Tragedy [Recorded by The Wombats]. On *Glitterbug* [Album]. 14th Floor, Bright Antenna.

New York hit-and-run laws: What to do if a driver leaves the scene. (2023). Enjuris. https://www.enjuris.com/new-york/car-accident/hit-and-run/

Norah, L. (2022, May 17). *Tips for driving in the USA.* Finding the Universe. https://www.findingtheuniverse.com/tips-for-driving-in-usa/

O'Barr, J. (1995). *The Crow.* Kitchen Sink Press.

PODS. (2019, April 2). *10 road trip survival tips for a cross-country move.* PODS Blog. https://www.pods.com/blog/2019/04/10-road-trip-survival-tips-for-a-cross-country-move/

The story of Smokey the Bear. (2014, August 4). U.S. Forest Service. https://www.fs.usda.gov/features/story-smokey-bear

Study reveals where drivers are most reliant on their GPS. (n.d.). United Tires Library. https://www.utires.com/articles/where-drivers-need-gps-the-most/

Swift, T. (2010). Speak Now [Recorded by Taylor Swift]. On *Speak Now* [Album]. Big Machine Records.

10 driving tips for new drivers. (2022). Bridgestone Tires. https://www.bridgestonetire.com/learn/maintenance/10-driving-tips-for-new-drivers/#

Tips for driving safely during the holiday season. (2022, November 18). Centers for Disease Control and Prevention. https://www.cdc.gov/injury/features/holiday-road-safety/index.html

Trcek, L. (2022, April 6). *Cross country road trip: 20 things to know before driving across the US.* Traveling Lifestyle. https://www.travelinglifestyle.net/7-things-to-consider-before-going-on-a-cross-country-road-trip-usa/

What to do after a car accident: Step-by-step guide. (2022, October). Allstate. https://www.allstate.com/resources/car-insurance/in-case-of-a-car-accident

What to do and expect when pulled over by law enforcement. (2023). American Association of Motor Vehicle Administrators. https://www.aamva.org/law-enforcement/what-to-do-when-stopped-by-law-enforcement

White, M. (2020, June 22). *10 road trip tips for driving across the country.* Moving.com. https://www.moving.com/tips/10-road-trip-tips-for-driving-across-the-country/

Why you should never leave the scene of an accident. (n.d.). Bernstein & Mello. https://www.bbmlawyers.com/why-you-should-never-leave-the-scene-of-an-accident/#:~:text=Flee-ing%20the%20scene%20of%20an,and%20call%20emergency%20services%20immediately.

Bibliography

Williams, A. (2020, June 22). *Dos and don'ts for your first US road trip*. A Dangerous Business Travel Blog. https://www.dangerous-business.com/dos-and-donts-on-a-great-american-road-trip/

Winter weather driving tips. (n.d.). United States Department of Transportation. https://www.nhtsa.gov/winter-driving-tips